W9-CCN-635

DISASTERS

1906 San Francisco
EARTHQUAKE

Tim Cooke

GARETH**STEVENS**
GS
PUBLISHING
A WRC Media Company

Please visit our web site at: **www.garethstevens.com**
For a free color catalog describing Gareth Stevens Publishing's list
of high-quality books and multimedia programs, call 1-800-542-2595 (USA)
or 1-800-387-3178 (Canada). Gareth Stevens Publishing's fax: (414) 332-3567.

Library of Congress Cataloging-in-Publication Data

Cooke, Tim (Tim A.)
    1906 San Francisco earthquake / Tim Cooke.
      p. cm. — (Disasters)
    Includes bibliographical references and index.
    ISBN 0-8368-4494-7 (lib. bdg.)
    1. San Francisco Earthquake, Calif., 1906— Juvenile literature.
  2. Earthquakes—California—San Francisco—Juvenile literature.
  I. Title. II. Disasters (Milwaukee, Wis.)
  QE536.2.U5C66 2005
  363.34'95'0979461—dc22   2004056707

This edition first published in 2005 by
Gareth Stevens Publishing
A WRC Media Company
330 West Olive Street, Suite 100
Milwaukee, Wisconsin 53212 USA

Original copyright © 2004 The Brown Reference Group plc. This U.S. edition
copyright © 2005 by Gareth Stevens, Inc.

Project Editor: Tim Cooke
Consultant: James A. Norwine, Professor of Geography, Texas A&M University
Designer: Lynne Ross
Picture Researcher: Becky Cox

Gareth Stevens series editor: Jenette Donovan Guntly
Gareth Stevens art direction: Tammy West

Picture credits: Front Cover: Corbis: Bettmann.
Corbis: Tom Bean 19, Bettmann title page, 20, 25, Hrafnsson Gisli Egill/Sygma 17, Roger
Ressmeyer 28, 29; Library of Congress: 5, 7, 8, 13, 21, 22–23, 23; National Archives:
6, 9, 10, 11, 12; Science Photo Library: GECO UK 24, James King-Holmes 18; Topham:
Picturepoint 27; Werner Foreman: 14.

Maps and Artwork: Brown Reference Group plc

Printed in the United States of America

1 2 3 4 5 6 7 8 9 09 08 07 06 05

ABOUT THE AUTHOR

Tim Cooke was educated at the University of Oxford. He has written
numerous reference books for older and younger readers. He lives
in London and works in publishing.

CONTENTS

1 DISASTER IN THE MORNING

San Francisco had been hit by many earthquakes in the nineteenth century, but they caused little damage. The city was still small at the time. By the late 1800s, San Francisco had grown large. The result was very different when an earthquake struck the city in spring 1906.

On the evening of April 17, 1906, the Italian singer Enrico Caruso sang at the Mission Opera House in San Francisco. He went to bed at the Palace Hotel. The next morning, he was woken soon after 5:00 A.M. when his bed began to rock. Outside, blocks of stone and brick were falling into the streets and people were screaming as an earthquake shook the city.

The singer got dressed quickly. He was terrified that the hotel would fall down. Not everyone had time to get dressed—many people ran into the streets in their pajamas. The earthquake set all the church bells ringing throughout the city.

A HUGE EARTHQUAKE

San Francisco had been hit by a powerful earthquake, which lasted about 45 to 60 seconds. People felt the ground shake all along the West Coast of the United States, from

▶ **This picture shows San Francisco after the earthquake and the fires that followed.**

4

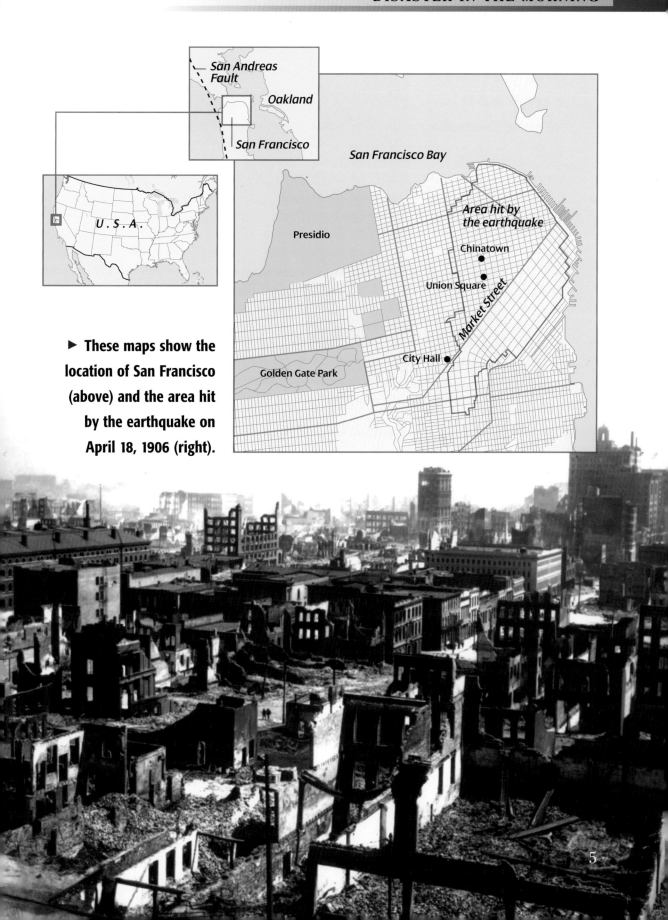

▶ These maps show the location of San Francisco (above) and the area hit by the earthquake on April 18, 1906 (right).

San Andreas Fault

Oakland

San Francisco

U.S.A.

San Francisco Bay

Presidio

Area hit by the earthquake

Chinatown

Union Square

Market Street

City Hall

Golden Gate Park

▶ **Wagons crowd a street in San Francisco as people rush to leave the city on the morning of the earthquake. The soldiers (bottom left) are on their way to help with the rescue.**

FACT FILE

WHERE:

U.S. West Coast from Los Angeles, California, to Oregon

WHEN:

5:13 A.M., April 18, 1906

TOTAL TIME:

45–60 seconds (main shock)

TOTAL STRENGTH:

8.3 on the Richter Scale

COSTS (approximate):

$400 million (1906 costs)

KILLED OR INJURED:

More than 3,000 people killed; 225,000 homeless

Oregon to Los Angeles, California, and east into Nevada. Damage was spread over about 12,000 square miles (31,000 square kilometers).

The worst damage was in San Francisco, which was home to 410,000 people. Many poor citizens lived in buildings on land that had once been part of the seabed of San Francisco Bay. The seabed had been drained to create more land for building. On the soft, muddy ground, whole buildings fell, burying people inside.

Elsewhere, the streets were full. Many people were trying to get to the **ferry port** to escape to Oakland, across the bay. Others headed for the railroad station. One witness said, "Automobiles piled high with bedding and hastily snatched stores tooted wild warnings amid the crowds."

At 8:14 A.M., reporter Fred J. Hewitt was near City Hall when a new **shock wave** struck. More buildings crashed down, including City Hall. Hewitt wrote, "Every person I saw was temporarily insane. A number of slight **tremors** followed the first shocks. As each came in turn . . . terror stamped its mark on every brow." In all, 135 aftershocks, or small tremors, followed the earthquake on April 18, 1906.

THE FIRES BEGIN

The city had no power. The earthquake had broken gas pipes and electricity wires and cracked water pipes. Then fires broke out

▼ **The rounded dome of City Hall's roof still stands after the earthquake. The rest of the building fell in a huge cloud of dust.**

► **Citizens crowd streets in San Francisco on the morning of the earthquake. The streets soon became blocked as people tried to flee the city.**

THE NERVOUS DOGS OF SAN FRANCISCO

Ernest S. Simpson was the editor of the *San Francisco Chronicle* newspaper. On the morning of April 18, 1906, he saw dogs running up the hill outside. *"They had come far, for they ran slowly. Their jaws were dripping. They moaned and they whined. All of them panted steadily up the steep hill. Then and thus I knew that . . . below us were nameless horrors, the dogs knew; and knowing, ran to the high places."*

and turned the sky dark. One man cried, "This must be the end of this wicked world."

Some of the fires that surrounded the city were caused by falling stoves and broken electrical wires. There were also underground explosions as broken gas pipes burst into flame. Fire spread quickly because many of the city's buildings were wooden. The noise of the huge fire was deafening. By 1:00 P.M., the whole of the downtown district was ablaze.

City officials moved quickly. U.S. Army troops based in the city joined firefighters and police to control the flames. There was no water, however, because of the broken pipes. The fire chief, Dennis Sullivan, had been a victim of the disaster. He died early in the day after being struck by falling stone. Without him, the firefighters did not know the location of the city's water cisterns, which are big tanks used to store water in case of emergencies. Instead, the firefighters decided to blow up buildings. They were trying to clear large gaps between the buildings that would serve as

GETTING NEWS OUT

The earthquake brought down most of San Francisco's telegraph and telephone wires. There was no way of getting news out to the rest of the country. Harry Jeffs, who was in charge of the telegraph wires at the Western Union Telegraph Company, went down by the bay. He climbed up and down dozens of telegraph poles until he found the break in the lines. He fixed it so he could send a telegram to the city of Sacramento. Jeffs sent out the first message about the disaster at 8:30 A.M. while sitting 30 feet (9 meters) up a pole. He stayed at his post for eighteen hours, repairing wires. The Western Union took over a cottage at the water's edge as an office. It had to send a huge number of telegrams as people tried to contact their family and friends.

▼ **A telegraph operator sends a message from an emergency desk outside City Hall. The earthquake made it unsafe to stay inside the building.**

▶ Firefighters try to rescue a victim buried beneath a house that had fallen down. Some firefighters were on duty for four or five days. They did not even have time to check to see if their own families were safe.

firebreaks. Even as they blew up the buildings, however, the flames found new ways around.

San Francisco's mayor, Eugene Schmitz, declared that anyone found looting would be shot. Looting is stealing from homes or stores left unguarded. Schmitz also created a group of fifty officials and citizens to run the city.

By the end of the first day, victims of the earthquake filled the city's **morgues**, and fires were burning throughout the city. Most San Franciscans were afraid more earthquakes would hit. They did not want to go back inside any buildings, so they settled down to sleep in city parks and on the beaches around San Francisco Bay. Many people would not return to their homes for weeks. People who escaped to Oakland ended up sleeping in a park. Enrico

Caruso slept on the ground in San Francisco's Union Square. The next morning, he found a cart to take him to the ferry.

RECOVERY OPERATION

Within twenty-four hours of the disaster, word spread beyond the city. The U.S. Army began sending tents and food to San Francisco. The army also took charge of health. With many people crowded together and no running water, there was a danger that diseases would spread. On April 20, 1906, President Theodore Roosevelt declared **martial law**, which put the military in charge of law and order. They set strict rules. People could not light candles in case it started another fire. One boy remembered that when his mother lit a stove to warm milk for his baby sister, a soldier told her, "Madam, put out that light and if you do that again I have to shoot you."

The fires raged for three days. By the time the firefighters finally got them under control, the fires had burned nearly five hundred city

▼ **A view of San Francisco before the earthquake struck. The city had grown quickly in the nineteenth century.**

11

► **These tents for people made homeless by the earthquake were set up in a San Francisco park by troops in the days following the disaster.**

blocks and 28,000 buildings. Some 225,000 people were homeless. Most of them lived in tents in parks.

EYEWITNESS

"We cooked our breakfast in the street, where rich and poor alike squat side by side cooking on brick stoves. Then all go stand in line to get their share of provisions. Everything left in stores has been distributed, and loads are coming in every day."

– *FREDERICK H. COLLINS*

SLOW RECOVERY

Nearly three-fourths of the city's residents had fled the city. As they returned, they put up notices asking for news of their missing family members. They offered rewards for information. Some families found their missing family members, but others were not so lucky.

Five days after the disaster, the homeless victims were soaked by a huge rainstorm. They did not have enough food or clean water until more supplies arrived. People had to dig holes in the streets to go to the bathroom. There were so many rats, which could carry disease, that city officials offered money for every rat that was killed.

THE CHINESE VICTIMS

Before the earthquake, San Francisco had a large Chinatown that was home to hundreds of Chinese people. Many Chinese people had first come to the West Coast to work. Many helped build the new railroads that crossed the United States. Many white San Franciscans did not want Chinese people in the city. When Chinatown burned down after the great earthquake, the white San Franciscans did not want it rebuilt.

Like other San Franciscans, the Chinese earthquake victims were homeless. They did not receive much comfort, however. Some residents complained that the Chinese smelled. In Berkeley, across the bay from San Francisco, residents put up signs reading "No Chinese" and "No Japanese." When the Chinese threatened to leave San Francisco, however, many San Franciscans did not want them to go. The Chinese were important because they ran a lot of trade with companies in Asia, which brought a lot of money to San Francisco. In the end, Chinatown stayed in San Francisco.

▼ **A Chinese resident prays amid the wreckage of Chinatown. Many San Franciscans wanted Chinese people to leave the city. They said that Chinese people were "uncivilized." In the end, the Chinese built a new Chinatown. It still stands today.**

2 THE CAUSES OF THE DISASTER

The damage in San Francisco had two main causes: the earthquake itself and the fire that followed. Studying the disaster gave experts a better understanding of why and where earthquakes happen.

In 1906, no one knew what caused earthquakes. They did not know why the ground moved. Ancient peoples believed that earthquakes were caused by demons or by gods who lived underground. By the year 1900, scientists believed that earthquakes were started by underground explosions.

COASTLINES

The discovery of the real cause of earthquakes came little by little. The first discovery came in 1912. A German scientist named Alfred Wegener noticed that the coastlines of some continents fit together like pieces of a jigsaw puzzle. Wegener guessed that the continents had once been

▼ **This statue is the Aztec god Tonatiuh. The Aztecs believed that Tonatiuh caused earthquakes.**

► This map shows how today's continents began to split up. They were once part of a huge continent named Pangaea, which started to split up between 100 and 200 million years ago. The continents have since drifted apart.

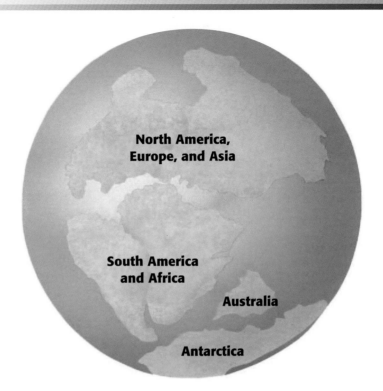

North America, Europe, and Asia

South America and Africa

Australia

Antarctica

joined together. He thought that the continents had slowly drifted apart over millions of years.

Scientists exploring the Atlantic Ocean in 1955 found a ridge of underwater mountains. The mountains were being created by **lava** that came up from underground and spread out on either side of the ridge. The lava was forming new ocean floor, and was also slowly pushing Europe, Africa, and the Americas farther apart. Wegener had been right: The continents do move, in a process called continental drift.

THE EARTH'S PLATES

By studying places with many earthquakes and volcanoes, scientists realized that Earth's surface is made of plates. These plates float on

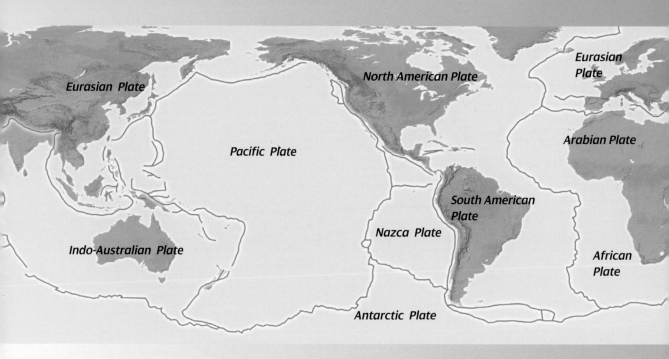

Eurasian Plate

North American Plate

Eurasian Plate

Eurasian Plate

Pacific Plate

Arabian Plate

South American Plate

Nazca Plate

Indo-Australian Plate

African Plate

Antarctic Plate

▲ **This map shows Earth's tectonic plates (tectonic means related to the crust of the planet). San Francisco stands near the place where the North American Plate and the Pacific Plate meet.**

a layer inside the earth called the mantle. In places, the mantle is made of rock so hot that it is a liquid called magma. Where two plates meet, the magma rises and cools to form new surface rock. In some places, one plate slides beneath another, back into the mantle. Often, this slide causes volcanoes, where melted rock bursts through Earth's surface as lava. Other plates hit and push up, creating mountains.

Most plates slide past one another by about 2 inches (5 centimeters) a year. If the plates jam together as they slide past one another, the rock stretches until it snaps back into shape. The sudden snap causes the earth to shake, which is called an earthquake.

The places where plates meet are called faults. Lands surrounding faults suffer many

◄ Smoke and ash rise from a volcano in Iceland at the northern end of the Mid-Atlantic Ridge, a fault where two of Earth's plates meet. Earthquakes happen where two plates grind together and stretch, then snap back into shape.

MEASURING EARTHQUAKES

Since the 1906 San Francisco earthquake, scientists have become skilled at measuring earthquakes. The most well-known scale, the Richter Scale, was created in 1935 by Charles Richter, a scientist from California. The scale measures the amount the ground shakes at different distances from the epicenter, which is the point where the earthquake begins. Each number on the scale, from 1 to 10, stands for an earthquake that is ten times more powerful than the previous number. The San Francisco earthquake rated 8.3 on the Richter Scale.

Today, most scientists use the moment **magnitude** scale, which more accurately measures large earthquakes. On this scale, the 1906 San Francisco earthquake rated about 7.7, a fairly high number.

▼ **A seismograph is a machine that measures shaking in the Earth. The shaking shows up as large squiggles in the lines.**

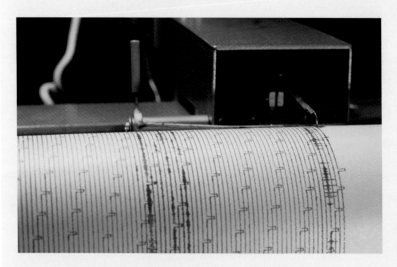

earthquakes. From the air, faults are easy to see. They create long, straight **ravines** and lakes. Sometimes, after the plates move, creeks, fences, or roads may zigzag a few feet to the left or right.

CALIFORNIA

San Francisco stands on the San Andreas Fault, which is a major fault that runs down the west

side of California. The fault has caused many earthquakes, including the 1906 San Francisco earthquake. Two other earthquakes that were just as strong happened along the fault in 1838 and 1868. In 1989, another earthquake struck. In the last 150 years, there have been six more earthquakes that were nearly as strong as these major events.

▲ **This photograph taken from an airplane shows the San Andreas Fault in California. The rocks on either side of the fault do not match up because they have slipped past each other over the centuries.**

In addition to the San Andreas Fault, California also has many smaller faults. Every year, thousands of earth tremors shake the state. Some scientists believe that one day, another huge earthquake will hit California.

EARTHQUAKE DAMAGE

One reason the earthquake of 1906 caused so much damage was that parts of San Francisco were built on land that had once been the seabed of San Francisco Bay. The land had been drained, but the muddy soil, called sediment, was weaker than rock. History had shown San Franciscans that this was not a good place to build. When an earthquake struck the city on

THE 1989 LOMA PRIETA EARTHQUAKE

A large earthquake hit San Francisco and the neighboring city of Oakland on Tuesday, October 17, 1989. The earthquake struck at 5:40 P.M., during the evening rush hour. The roads were full of people going home from work. About sixty-two thousand fans were crowded into San Francisco's Candlestick Park for a World Series baseball game between the San Francisco Giants and the Oakland A's. The game was stopped after the earthquake struck.

Although fires broke out in parts of San Francisco, firefighters soon put them out. About twenty thousand buildings were damaged, but not many buildings fell down. Compared to 1906, few people were hurt. About sixty people died. Most deaths happened on a raised part of Interstate 880 in Oakland. The road collapsed, killing people trapped in their cars.

▼ **Players and fans rush onto the field at Candlestick Park after the 1989 Loma Prieta earthquake. The safest place to be was on the playing field in case the stadium fell down.**

October 21, 1868, **engineers** saw that buildings on the soft land were more likely to fall down. They also saw that falling stone from buildings was very dangerous. By 1906, most people had forgotten these lessons, however.

► Smoke rises from burning buildings in San Francisco in the background of this photograph. The picture was taken on April 18, 1906, the day of the earthquake, after fires broke out all over the city.

FIRE AND ARSON

After the earthquake, most damage in the city was caused by fires. Small fires joined into one huge fire, and the firefighters did not have enough water to put out such a large blaze.

Some people started fires on purpose, which is called arson. They set fire to their own property to get insurance money. People buy insurance on valuable items, such as houses. If their property is damaged, the insurance company pays them money to make repairs or buy new property. Insurance companies did not pay for earthquake damage, but they would pay for damage caused by fires.

Some owners of homes and businesses whose property fell down in the earthquake set fire to the ruins. They hoped that insurers would think that the damage had been caused by the fire and would pay for the repairs.

21

3 LIVING WITH EARTHQUAKES

Despite the damage and many deaths, the 1906 San Francisco earthquake helped people prepare for future disasters. It led to changes in the study of earthquakes. The disaster also led to new building laws that helped make the city safer.

Within San Francisco, work was soon under way to rebuild structures such as City Hall. People began to return to their homes, or to rebuild them. They still faced many problems. In 1907, for example, lack of good ways to clear trash and waste led to many cases of a serious disease called the bubonic plague. The disease was spread by fleas living in the fur of rats. Throughout the twentieth century, however, many new buildings were built in San Francisco, mainly in the downtown district. A new Chinatown was built near the downtown area. It is now a great attraction for visitors.

▼ **This view of San Francisco was taken in 1909. Much of the city had been rebuilt in the three years since the disaster.**

LESSONS FROM THE EARTHQUAKE

There is no way to stop earthquakes, but the 1906 earthquake taught useful lessons about how to deal with them. Since that time, San Francisco officials have planned how to better deal with an earthquake. One important task was to rebuild the water system so that there would always be water supplies for firefighters. Another task was to create laws called building codes. The laws made sure that new structures were built to high safety standards. Other laws stopped the crowding together of wooden buildings, which would burn easily. In 1972, a new law stopped schools, hospitals, power plants, or homes from being built near earthquake faults.

▲ A new City Hall was built on the site of the old one. In the background of this image is the original dome, which survived the earthquake.

▶ **A geologist in California sets up a seismograph. More than one thousand machines check movements of the ground in California. The machines help give scientists warnings so they can be ready if another large earthquake hits.**

Another guard against earthquakes is learning how to predict them better. The 1906 earthquake led to interest in seismology, which is the study of earthquakes. After the 1906 earthquake, Andrew C. Lawson, a professor at the University of California, created the State Earthquake Investigation Commission. The group included twenty scientists who gathered information on the earthquake. They noted why some buildings stood up to the shock waves better than others and which parts of the city offered stronger ground for building. Their report helped improve building designs. Other scientists walked the length of the San Andreas Fault to measure how far it had

SURVIVING EARTHQUAKES

Children who live in earthquake areas, such as California, practice drills at school so that they know what to do if an earthquake happens. Most people are injured by falling walls and windows, so it is better to stay away from the outer walls of buildings. The safest thing to do, if possible, is to drop to the floor and take cover under a solid desk or table until the shaking stops. Hold on to a leg of the table so that it does not move away from you. If you are not near a table or desk, you should cover your head with your arms to protect it from any falling objects. If you are in bed, stay there and cover your head with a pillow for protection. If you are outside when an earthquake hits, stay outside. Try to move to a clear area with no buildings, trees, or road signs that might fall and injure you.

▼ **Students in Parkfield, California, practice an earthquake drill in their classroom. The town has more earth tremors than anywhere else in the United States.**

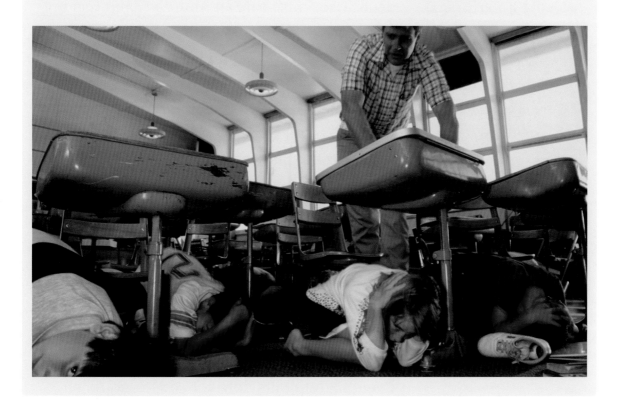

slipped. In some places it had moved by as much as 20 feet (6 m), creating breaks in fences and creeks.

PREDICTING EARTHQUAKES

Today, California has more than one thousand seismographs. Since 1977, the study of earthquakes has been the duty of the U.S. Geological Survey (USGS). Geologists believe that they will see signs of a large earthquake in time to get people out of dangerous areas. They believe the San Andreas Fault running underneath San Francisco suffers a major earthquake about once every two hundred years, so another earthquake is due around 2106. The Southern San Andreas Fault has not had a major event since 1857. An earthquake may happen there sooner.

One place that geologists study is Parkfield, California. The town has suffered a somewhat weak earthquake every twenty to twenty-two years for the last century. That makes Parkfield the earthquake capital of the United States.

EARTHQUAKE-PROOF BUILDINGS

People often ask seismologists what sort of building they would like to be inside during an earthquake. They expect the answer to be something strong like steel, concrete, or wood. The scientists usually like to reply, "A tent." Even if a tent falls down, it causes no damage.

THE WHOLE STORY

Gladys Hansen looked after San Francisco's records. In the 1980s and 1990s, Hansen studied records to discover the real story of the 1906 earthquake. She found that the number of people who died was three to four times more than the official total of about seven hundred.

Hansen wondered why the official number was so low. She thought people may have tried to make the disaster seem less serious than it really was. It may have been city officials, who had wanted people to keep investing in San Francisco. Also, Hansen thought that photographs may have been changed to make the damage look less severe.

PROTECTING THE GOLDEN GATE BRIDGE

One of San Francisco's greatest tourist sights, which may suffer from a future earthquake, is the Golden Gate Bridge. It was built to withstand an earthquake of about 7.0 on the Richter scale. A more powerful shock might make the bridge fall down.

In the late 1990s, engineers began to work to make the bridge stronger. They strengthened the bases of the towers that hold the bridge up. Engineers also worked to join the separate spans of the roadway so that they would move as one piece. The north **viaduct** work was completed in April 2002. The south viaduct work is more difficult and will take four more years to complete. The work is difficult because it all has to be done without stopping traffic. After the work, the bridge will be able to survive a tremor of up to 8.3 on the Richter scale.

▼ **The Golden Gate Bridge is not only a symbol of San Francisco, it is also part of an important route from the city to other places in northern California.**

Understanding earthquakes has helped architects develop ways to protect buildings from earthquakes. Buildings now have springy parts in their bases made of layers of steel and rubber or plastic. When the Earth shakes, the buildings do not move as much. The bases have been used in California since 1985 to protect some new buildings. Older buildings can also be fitted with the bases, but it is a long, expensive job. It is easier to put guards in the first time, rather than add them later.

Protecting buildings is important for the future. It is likely that one day another major earthquake will hit California. When that happens, the more buildings that are protected when the earthquake hits, the fewer people will be in danger of being hurt or killed.

▼ **This photograph shows downtown San Francisco at the end of the twentieth century. Most of the city's tall buildings are now earthquake proof.**

TESTING BUILDINGS

Improving buildings so that they can survive earthquakes is slow work. Most architects can only plan a building that they think might not fall down during an earthquake and build it. Usually the process includes strengthening the base on which the building stands. Then the architects just have to wait to see what happens to the building in an earthquake—if an earthquake happens at all. This way of building might all change with a program begun in the United States at the start of the twenty-first century. U.S. scientists plan to create a "shake table" that is 1,000 square feet (93 square m) large. The table will be strong enough to support buildings up to ten stories tall. It will be able to shake them in the same way an earthquake would. The table will allow scientists to test the results of different building methods to avoid earthquake damage without waiting for a real disaster to strike.

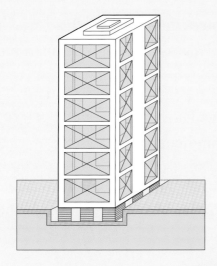

▲ This drawing shows a building with a rubber and steel base. The springy base absorbs movement during an earthquake.

► This house has been built on a "shake table" to test its strength during an earthquake.

GLOSSARY

engineers People who are trained to work with engines or to make or build things.

ferry port A building on a river or coast from which passenger boats make regular trips to other places.

firebreaks Empty spaces that are created in the path of a fire to stop the flames from spreading, because there is nothing to burn.

geologist Person who studies soil, rocks, and minerals and what they tell us about the history of Earth.

lava Melted rock after it has come out of the ground and which is so hot that it is a thick liquid. Lava also describes the rock when it has cooled and hardened on Earth's surface.

magnitude The strength of the force of an earthquake's shock waves and the area affected.

martial law Emergency laws that are enforced by military officials and not by the police or courts that usually uphold the law.

morgues Places where dead bodies are kept until officials have learned who the dead person is.

ravines Deep, narrow valleys that are somewhat like canyons.

shock waves Shaking movements like ripples that travel through the ground after an earthquake.

telegraph A machine for sending messages by wires or radio over long distances.

tremors Short periods of shaking movements that often follow an earthquake. Tremors are usually not as violent as the main shocks.

viaduct A bridge used to hold up a road or railroad crossing over a valley, highway, river, or other body of water.

FURTHER RESEARCH

BOOKS

Brunelle, Lynn. *Earthquake!: The 1906 San Francisco Nightmare (X-Treme Disasters That Changed America)*. Bearport, 2005.

Meister, Cari. *Earthquakes (Nature's Fury)*. Abdo and Daughters Publishing, 1999.

Sherrow, Victoria. *"San Francisco Earthquake, 1989: Death and Destruction" (American Disasters)*. Enslow Publishers, 1998.

Sipiera, Paul P. *Earthquakes (True Books: Nature)*. Children's Press, 1998.

WEB SITES

Earthquake Shake
www.thetech.org/exhibits_events/online/quakes/

Earthquakes for Kids
earthquakes.usgs.gov/4kids/

The Great 1906 San Francisco Earthquake, United States Geological Survey
quake.wr.usgs.gov/info/1906/index.html

Life Along the Faultline
www.exploratorium.com/faultline/index.html

Putting Down Roots in Earthquake Country
www.earthquakecountry.info/roots/contents.html

Savage Earth
www.pbs.org/wnet/savageearth/